HOW TO SELL ON LINKEDIN 2023

USING LINKEDIN FOR BUSINESS, SALES AND MARKETING

By Ella Nelson

Click here to get another self help book on selling on Etsy

Click here to get a self help book on selling on ebay

Table of Contents.

About The Author.

Ella Nelson is a seasoned professional with a remarkable track record in the world of sales, business development, and social networking. With a *few* years of experience in helping businesses thrive and individuals achieve their career aspirations, Ella Nelson brings a wealth of knowledge and passion to the art of selling on LinkedIn.

What sets Ella Nelson apart is her unwavering commitment to empowering others. She have successfully guided countless individuals and organizations on harnessing the immense potential of LinkedIn as a powerful sales and networking platform. The impact of her guidance can be seen in the stories of professionals who have turned leads into clients, connections into lasting relationships, and potential into tangible results.

In this book, Ella Nelson distills her years of experience into actionable strategies that anyone can implement. Her approach is not only practical but also deeply rooted in a profound understanding of the dynamics of LinkedIn, sales psychology, and effective communication. She believes that success on LinkedIn is not just about selling but about building meaningful and mutually beneficial connections.

With an engaging writing style, Ella Nelson takes complex concepts and distills them into easy-to-understand, step-by-step guides. Her ability to blend practical advice with motivational insights is what makes her writing resonate with readers. The book not only equips you with the tools to excel on LinkedIn but also instills the confidence and drive to take your sales game to the next level.

Ella Nelson is not just a writer and expert but also a dedicated mentor and lifelong learner. She stays at the forefront of the ever-evolving LinkedIn landscape, constantly adapting and experimenting with new strategies. She believes that one's journey toward success is never truly complete, and She inspire others to embrace a similar mindset.

As you embark on this LinkedIn sales journey with Ella Nelson, you are not just learning from an accomplished professional; you are learning from a mentor who is deeply invested in your success. This book is not just a manual; it's a testament to what is possible when passion meets knowledge and hard work meets opportunity.

So, dive into the pages of this book with confidence and excitement. With Ella Nelson as your guide, you are on the path to discovering the true potential of LinkedIn and unlocking your own success story. Let's embark on this journey together and transform your LinkedIn experience into a powerful sales engine for your career or business.

Introduction

In a world driven by digital connectivity and professional networking, the value of an effective LinkedIn presence cannot be overstated. Welcome to "How to sell on LinkedIn 2023," your roadmap to harnessing the full potential of this powerful platform. In the following pages, you will embark on a transformative journey that will enable you to craft an impactful LinkedIn profile and leverage it for your business, sales, and marketing aspirations.

LinkedIn, the virtual professional playground, has rapidly evolved from a simple resume repository to a thriving ecosystem where business deals are sealed, careers are forged, and market influence is cultivated. This book is your gateway to this dynamic world, offering you not only the knowledge to create a compelling LinkedIn profile but also the strategies to thrive in the realm of entrepreneurship, sales, and marketing.

The LinkedIn Revolution: A Prelude to Success

We live in an era where information is exchanged at the speed of light, and connections are formed with just a click. As a professional, entrepreneur, marketer, or salesperson, the keys to success lie in your ability to navigate this digital landscape effectively. With over 774 million professionals worldwide, LinkedIn is your gateway to a vast network of opportunities, making it one of the most influential platforms for business, sales, and marketing.

LinkedIn is more than just an online resume; it's your digital business card, your online portfolio, and your professional identity, all rolled into one. It's the platform where opportunities come knocking, partnerships are forged, and deals are sealed. However, your success on LinkedIn hinges on how you present yourself, how you interact, and how you leverage the vast array of tools it offers.

Crafting Your Digital Persona

Your LinkedIn profile is not merely a static document but a dynamic reflection of your professional journey, your skills, and your aspirations. Within the pages of this book, you'll learn how to construct an engaging, professional narrative that captivates your audience and compels them to connect, engage, and do business with you.

But it doesn't stop there. "How to sell on LinkedIn 2023" is not a mere profile-building tutorial. It's a comprehensive manual that takes you beyond the basics and delves into the heart of LinkedIn's marketing and sales potential. We'll unravel the mysteries of content marketing, show you how to generate leads, build your brand's online presence, and unveil strategies that will set you on the path to becoming a LinkedIn influencer.

Sales, Marketing, and Beyond

For businesses, LinkedIn offers a treasure trove of opportunities. Whether you're an entrepreneur looking to grow your startup, a sales professional aiming to build a lucrative client base, or a marketer seeking to reach a broader audience, LinkedIn provides the tools and strategies necessary to achieve your goals.

With advanced features like Sales Navigator and sponsored content, you can identify, connect, and engage with potential clients in a highly targeted and effective manner. For marketers, LinkedIn's advertising options are a goldmine for reaching a niche audience. The power of LinkedIn Groups and Events cannot be underestimated, allowing you to establish thought leadership and position your brand for success.

But the real question is, are you ready to unleash the full potential of LinkedIn? Are you prepared to transform your profile into a dynamic marketing tool and your network into a vibrant community of clients and collaborators.

Unleash Your Potential

The journey to LinkedIn success begins with your commitment to learn, adapt, and grow. In the pages that follow, you'll gain insights, strategies, and a wealth of knowledge to transform your LinkedIn profile into a powerhouse of business, sales, and marketing. But knowledge alone is not enough; action is the catalyst of success.

Are you ready to take that step? Are you prepared to unlock the door to unprecedented opportunities in the digital age? Don't just read this book – implement its strategies and watch your LinkedIn journey unfold. Join the ranks of professionals who have harnessed the immense potential of LinkedIn for their business, sales, and marketing success. Your success story starts now.

So, are you ready to unleash your potential and transform your LinkedIn experience? Let's dive in and unlock the world of opportunities that awaits. Your journey to LinkedIn excellence begins now.

"Your network is your net worth." - Porter Gale

This quote emphasizes the importance of building a strong professional network, which is a fundamental aspect of successful selling on LinkedIn.

"The biggest mistake in sales and marketing is to focus on features and benefits. The most important thing is to listen." - Alex Alexandrou

Effective sales on LinkedIn involves active listening and understanding your prospects' needs and challenges before presenting solutions.

Chapter 1

Setting up your LinkedIn profile

LinkedIn is a powerful platform for networking, job hunting, and business development. To maximize its potential, creating a well-optimized profile is crucial. Here is a well detailed guidelines to follow to set up your pathway to success.

Sign Up and Start Your Profile:

Go to LinkedIn's homepage **(www.linkedin.com)** and click "Join now" or "Sign up."

Fill in your first and last name, email address, and a secure password.

Click "Join now" or "Agree & Join" if you agree with LinkedIn's Terms of Service and Privacy Policy.

Profile Basics:

After signing up, LinkedIn will guide you through profile basics. These include uploading a profile picture and adding basic information.

Upload a professional profile photo. It should be a clear headshot with a neutral background, where you appear approachable and professional.

Customize Your LinkedIn URL:

Click on "Edit public profile & URL" on the right-hand side of your profile.

Under "Edit your custom URL," click the "Edit" icon and create a customized, professional URL (e.g., www.linkedin.com/in/yourname).

Create a Headline:

Your headline is a concise description of your professional identity. It appears below your name. Craft a headline that summarizes your role and expertise. For example, "Digital Marketing Specialist" or "Sales Professional | Helping Businesses Grow."

Write Your Summary:

In the "About" section, write a compelling summary about yourself. Highlight your skills, achievements, and career goals. Use keywords relevant to your industry to increase your profile's visibility.

Add Experience:

In the "Experience" section, list your work history.

Include your job title, company, dates of employment, and a brief description of your role and accomplishments.

Add media (e.g., presentations, projects) to showcase your work.

Education and Certifications:

Include details about your educational background and any relevant certifications.

Mention your degree, major, school name, and graduation year.

Skills and Endorsements:

List your skills in the "Skills & Endorsements" section.

Seek endorsements from colleagues and connections to validate your skills.

Recommendations:

Request recommendations from former colleagues or supervisors. These personalized testimonials add credibility to your profile.

Accomplishments:

- In this section, you can add additional information like publications, languages, volunteer experiences, and more. Highlight any publications, patents, courses, and other notable achievements under "Accomplishments."

Contact and Personal Info:

- Fill in your contact information and personal details. Make sure your contact details are up to date.

Profile and Network Visibility:

- Customize your profile's visibility settings. You can choose who can see your connections, your activity feed, and more.

Privacy Settings:

- Review and adjust your privacy settings according to your preferences, including who can see your activity and personal information.

Profile Completeness:

- LinkedIn provides a profile strength meter. Strive for a "All-Star" profile status by adding all relevant details.

Connections:

- Start building your network by connecting with colleagues, friends, and acquaintances. Personalize connection requests when possible.

Engage with Content:

- Start engaging with posts, articles, and updates from your network to build your presence and establish credibility.

Follow Companies and Influencers:

- Follow companies and thought leaders in your industry to stay updated on trends and opportunities.

Showcase Your Work:

- Use the "Featured" section to showcase projects, articles, and other work you're proud of.

Get Endorsed:

- Actively endorse your connections' skills, and they're likely to reciprocate.

Stay Active:

- Keep your profile updated with new accomplishments, experiences, and skills.

Personalizing Your Profile

"Your LinkedIn profile is your digital business card and professional brand. Personalizing it not only makes a lasting first impression but also enhances your visibility and credibility in the professional world."

Step-by-Step Guide to Personalizing Your LinkedIn Profile:

Profile Picture:

Upload a professional headshot with a neutral background.

Your face should be clearly visible, and you should appear approachable and well-groomed.

Custom LinkedIn URL:

Click on "Edit public profile & URL" on the right-hand side.

Under "Edit your custom URL," click the "Edit" icon and create a customized, professional URL (e.g., www.linkedin.com/in/yourname).

Headline:

Craft a headline that succinctly describes your professional identity.

Use keywords related to your field or industry to make your profile more discoverable.

Summary:

In the "About" section, write a captivating summary that tells your professional story.

Highlight your skills, achievements, and aspirations.

Use keywords to boost your profile's searchability.

Experience:

List your work history, including job titles, company names, employment dates, and descriptions of your roles.

Add media, such as project links or presentations, to showcase your work.

Education and Certifications:

Include information about your educational background, including degrees, majors, institutions, and graduation years.

Mention relevant certfications and licenses.

Skills and Endorsements:

List your key skills.

Encourage connections to endorse your skills to validate your expertise.

Recommendations:

Request recommendations from former colleagues, supervisors, or clients.

Personalized testimonials add credibility to your profile.

Accomplishments:

In this section, include publications, patents, courses, and other notable achievements.

Share links or details about your accomplishments.

Contact and Personal Info:

Fill in your contact information and personal details. Ensure that your contact details are current and accurate.

Profile and Network Visibility:

Customize profile visibility settings, including who can see your connections and activity feed.

Privacy Settings:

Review and adjust your privacy settings, such as who can see your activity and personal information.

Profile Completeness:

Strive for an "All-Star" profile status by completing all relevant sections of your profile.

Connections:

Start building your network by connecting with colleagues, friends, and acquaintances.

Personalize connection requests when possible.

Engage with Content:

Interact with posts, articles, and updates from your network to build your presence and establish credibility.

Follow Companies and Influencers:

Follow companies and thought leaders in your industry to stay updated on trends and opportunities.

Showcase Your Work:

Use the "Featured" section to display projects, articles, and other work you're proud of.

Get Endorsed:

Actively endorse your connections' skills, and they're likely to reciprocate.

Request Recommendations:

Ask colleagues, supervisors, and clients for written recommendations to add to your profile.

Stay Active:

Keep your profile updated with new accomplishments, experiences, and skills.

You will personalize your LinkedIn profile to stand out and make a strong professional impression. Your well-optimized profile will help you connect with peers, expand your network, and seize new opportunities in your field.

Building Your Network on LinkedIn

LinkedIn is a dynamic platform where professional connections and relationships flourish. To leverage its full potential, nurturing a strong and diverse network is paramount. Before connecting with others, ensure your profile is complete and professional. Your profile picture, headline, and summary play a vital role in creating a strong first impression.

Begin by connecting with current and former colleagues. They are the foundation of your LinkedIn network and can introduce you to their connections. When sending connection requests, always include a personal note. Mention how you know the person or why you'd like to connect. Personalization goes a long way in building rapport. Regularly engage with your network's content by liking, commenting, and sharing. This not only keeps you visible but also helps you stay connected with your contacts.

Participate in LinkedIn groups relevant to your field or interests. These communities are excellent places to meet like-minded professionals and share insights. LinkedIn offers various virtual events, from webinars to industry meet-ups. Attending these can lead to new connections and valuable conversations. Initiate conversations with your connections. Share your knowledge, ask for advice, and express your genuine interest in building a professional relationship.

Ask for recommendations from colleagues, supervisors, or clients. These endorsements validate your skills and expertise. If you're a part of any educational institution, connect with alumni from your alma mater. Shared experiences can be the basis for meaningful connections. Following and connecting with industry influencers can provide you with valuable insights and access to their networks.

Always maintain professionalism and respect in your interactions. Your reputation on LinkedIn matters just as it does in the real world. Be generous with your knowledge and support. Offer help and resources to your network before seeking assistance.

Remember, building a network on LinkedIn is an ongoing process. It's not just about quantity but the quality of your connections. Building meaningful relationships can open doors to opportunities, career growth, and valuable collaborations. So, stay engaged, be authentic, and watch your professional network thrive.

Showcasing Your Expertise on LinkedIn

LinkedIn isn't just a platform for connecting with professionals; it's also a powerful stage for showcasing your expertise and becoming a thoughtful leader in your industry. Whether you're seeking new opportunities, aiming to grow your business, or simply want to share your knowledge, here's how you can effectively demonstrate your expertise on LinkedIn.

1. Create Engaging Content:

Share your insights, experiences, and valuable content. Write and share articles, posts, and updates related to your field. By consistently offering valuable information, you position yourself as a knowledgeable resource.

2. Visual Portfolio:

Use the "Featured" section on your profile to display your work, such as projects, presentations, and articles. Visual representations of your accomplishments can leave a lasting impression.

3. Be Active in Groups:

Join LinkedIn groups relevant to your industry or interests. Engage in discussions, offer solutions, and share your expertise. Groups provide an excellent platform for networking and showcasing your knowledge.

4. Connect with Influencers:

Follow and connect with thought leaders and influencers in your field. Engage with their content and join discussions. This not only keeps you informed but also increases your visibility.

5. Share Success Stories:

Don't shy away from sharing your achievements and success stories. Highlight the projects you've worked on, the problems you've solved, and the impact you've made.

6. Offer Solutions:

If you come across questions or problems posted by your connections, provide thoughtful solutions or guidance. This not only showcases your expertise but also demonstrates your willingness to help.

7. Write Thoughtful Recommendations:

Write recommendations for your connections when they've delivered excellent work. In turn, they're likely to reciprocate. Thoughtful recommendations highlight your expertise.

8. Maintain a Professional Blog:

Consider writing a blog on LinkedIn. Share your industry insights, trends, and experiences. A well-maintained blog can attract a following and establish your authority.

9. Share Industry News:

Stay updated on the latest industry news and share relevant articles. Offer your perspective on the news to showcase your understanding of the industry landscape.

10. Engage with Your Network:

Respond to comments on your posts and engage with others' content. These interactions help in creating a dynamic, supportive network.

11. Seek Speaking Opportunities:

If you're comfortable with public speaking, seek out opportunities to present at webinars or events. Share the recorded sessions on LinkedIn.

12. Collaborate and Network:

Collaborate with other professionals, especially those in complementary fields. Networking and joint projects can expand your reach and reinforce your expertise.

Remember, showcasing your expertise on LinkedIn is not about self-promotion but about providing value and insight to your network. By consistently sharing your knowledge, offering solutions, and engaging with your connections, you'll be seen as a valuable resource and an authority in your field.

"The best salespeople on LinkedIn don't sell; they tell stories, solve problems, and share insights." - Jill Rowley

Modern sales on LinkedIn often involves storytelling, problem-solving, and providing valuable insights rather than traditional sales pitches.

Chapter 2

Content Marketing on LinkedIn

Content marketing on LinkedIn is a dynamic strategy for professionals, businesses, and brands looking to connect with their target audience, build relationships, and establish themselves as thought leaders in their industry. With over 774 million professionals worldwide, LinkedIn is a prime platform for sharing valuable content and engaging with a like-minded audience. Here's a comprehensive look at content marketing on LinkedIn and how to make it work for you.

The Power of Content Marketing:

Content marketing involves creating and sharing informative, relevant, and valuable content to attract and engage a specific audience. On LinkedIn, this approach is tailored to a professional context, aiming to educate, inspire, and connect with other professionals. The benefits of content marketing on LinkedIn are multifaceted:

Establish Authority: Sharing insightful content positions you as an expert in your field, building trust among your connections and followers.

Grow Your Network: Valuable content encourages others to connect with you, expanding your reach and network.

Drive Engagement: Informative and thought-provoking content sparks discussions and interactions, increasing your visibility.

Foster Brand Awareness: By consistently sharing your brand's message, you reinforce your brand identity and increase brand recognition.

Generate Leads: High-quality content attracts potential clients, partners, and opportunities.

Content Types:

LinkedIn offers various content formats to showcase your expertise and engage your audience:

- ➢ **Articles:** Publish long-form articles that delve deep into topics, share insights, and provide practical advice.
- ➢ **Posts:** Short updates that can include text, images, links, or videos. Ideal for sharing quick updates, thoughts, or links to external content.
- ➢ **Documents and Media:** Share presentations, documents, or videos to support your narrative and visually showcase your work.

Content Creation Tips:

Creating effective content on LinkedIn involves the following best practices:

- ➢ **Know Your Audience:** Understand the needs and interests of your target audience. Tailor your content to address their pain points and questions.
- ➢ **Consistency:** Regular posting keeps your audience engaged. Create a content calendar to maintain consistency.
- ➢ **Use Visuals:** Incorporate images, infographics, and videos to make your content visually appealing and shareable.

- ➤ **Engage and Interact:** Respond to comments on your posts, join discussions, and engage with your connections' content. Networking is an essential part of content marketing.

- ➤ **Data-Driven Approach:** Analyze the performance of your content using LinkedIn analytics. Adjust your strategy based on what works best for your audience.

- ➤ **Call to Action (CTA):** Encourage your audience to take a specific action, such as liking, sharing, commenting, or visiting your website.

- ➤ **Be Authentic:** Share personal experiences and stories to connect with your audience on a more emotional level.

Measuring Success:

LinkedIn provides analytics tools to measure the performance of your content. Track metrics like engagement rate, click-through rate, and follower growth to gauge the effectiveness of your content marketing efforts.

Content marketing on LinkedIn is an influential approach to building your professional brand, connecting with your audience, and achieving your business goals. By creating and sharing valuable content, engaging with your network, and staying authentic, you can harness the full potential of this platform and solidify your presence as an industry expert.

Creating Engaging Posts on LinkedIn

LinkedIn, the professional networking platform, offers a valuable opportunity to share insights, connect with your target audience, and establish your expertise. Creating engaging posts on LinkedIn is a powerful way to achieve these goals and elevate your professional presence. LinkedIn is a place to know how to craft posts that captivate your audience and foster meaningful interactions.

Know Your Audience:

Before you start creating posts, it's essential to understand your target audience. Who are you trying to reach, and what are their interests and pain points? Tailor your content to address their needs and engage them effectively.

Quality Over Quantity:

While consistency is important, quality should always be the priority. It's better to create fewer, high-quality posts that resonate with your audience than to flood your feed with content that doesn't add value.

Post Types:

LinkedIn offers various post formats, including text, images, videos, links, documents, and polls. Use a mix of these to keep your content fresh and engaging. Visual content, such as images and videos, tends to perform well and capture attention.

Headlines Matter:

Craft attention-grabbing headlines. They should be concise and intriguing, sparking curiosity and encouraging readers to click, like, comment, and share. Use keywords that are relevant to your industry to improve discoverability.

Inform, Inspire, or Educate:

Your posts should aim to inform, inspire, or educate your audience. Share industry insights, success stories, or practical tips. Thought-provoking content often leads to more engagement.

Clear and Concise:

Keep your posts clear and concise. While LinkedIn allows for longer-form content, it's essential to make your point succinctly and effectively. Use short paragraphs and bullet points to enhance readability.

Visual Appeal:

Visual elements like images and videos capture attention. Use relevant images to complement your posts or embed videos that provide further context. Visual appeal encourages people to stop scrolling and engage with your content.

Call to Action (CTA):

End your posts with a clear and compelling call to action. Encourage your audience to like, share, comment, visit your website, or take another desired action. A well-crafted CTA can boost engagement.

Engage with Your Audience:

Engagement isn't a one-way street. Respond to comments on your posts, join discussions, and interact with your connections' content. Engaging with your audience builds relationships and strengthens your professional network.

Consistency:

Create a posting schedule and stick to it. Consistency keeps your audience engaged and expecting your content. However, it's important to maintain quality even when posting frequently.

Analytics:

LinkedIn provides analytics tools that allow you to measure the performance of your posts. Track metrics like reach, engagement, and click-through rates to understand what resonates with your audience. Adjust your strategy based on these insights.

In conclusion, crafting engaging posts on LinkedIn is an art and science. By knowing your audience, maintaining quality, using the right post types, and adhering to best practices, you can create content that captures attention, sparks meaningful conversations, and elevates your professional presence on the platform.

Sharing Valuable Content on LinkedIn

LinkedIn is not just a platform for professional networking; it's also a treasure trove of valuable content. To leverage the full potential of this platform, it's crucial to share content that educates, inspires, and engages your audience. Whether you're a professional seeking to establish thought leadership or a business looking to connect with your target market.

Before diving into content creation, it's essential to know your target audience. Who are they? What are their interests and pain points? Tailoring your content to their needs is the key to engagement.

LinkedIn offers various content formats – from text-based posts and articles to images, videos, documents, and polls. Utilize a mix of these formats to keep your content fresh and appealing to a broader audience. Visual content, such as images and videos, is particularly effective in capturing attention. The best content typically falls into one of these categories: it informs, inspires, or educates. Share industry insights, success stories, practical tips, and thought-provoking ideas. By offering value, you're more likely to engage your audience.

In a world where attention spans are short, it's vital to keep your content clear and concise. While LinkedIn does allow for longer-form content, it's crucial to make your point succinctly and effectively. Break up your text into short paragraphs and use bullet points for readability. Visual elements, such as images and videos, can greatly enhance your content's appeal. Use relevant images to complement your posts, or embed videos that provide additional context. Visual content not only captures attention but also encourages people to engage with your posts.

Craft compelling headlines that grab your audience's attention. Your headlines should be concise, intriguing, and relevant. They play a pivotal role in whether readers choose to engage with your content. LinkedIn is a platform where you can showcase your expertise. Share your professional experiences, insights, and success stories. By demonstrating your knowledge and skills, you'll establish credibility in your field. Sharing content isn't just a one-way street. Actively engage with your audience by responding to comments on your posts and participating in discussions. Interacting with your connections fosters relationships and strengthens your professional network.

Conclude your content with a clear and compelling call to action. Encourage your audience to like, share, comment, visit your website, or take another desired action. A well-crafted CTA (call to action) can significantly boost engagement. Develop a posting schedule and stick to it. Consistency keeps your audience engaged and looking forward to your content. It's essential to maintain quality even when posting frequently.

LinkedIn provides analytics tools that enable you to track the performance of your content. Pay attention to metrics like reach, engagement, and click-through rates to understand what resonates with your audience. Use these insights to refine your content strategy.

In conclusion, sharing valuable content on LinkedIn is a strategic endeavor that blends art and science. By understanding your audience, diversifying content formats, providing value, and adhering to best practices, you can effectively share content that educates, inspires, and engages your professional network, ultimately elevating your presence on the platform.

Harnessing Recommendations on LinkedIn: Building Credibility and Trust

LinkedIn recommendations are powerful endorsements from colleagues, supervisors, clients, or partners that vouch for your professional skills and character. These recommendations serve as a testament to your expertise, reliability, and integrity. When harnessed effectively, LinkedIn recommendations can play a pivotal role in building credibility, trust, and a strong professional brand.

1. Why Recommendations Matter:

LinkedIn recommendations are more than just digital pats on the back. They are valuable assets that can significantly boost your professional profile in various ways:

- **Credibility:** Recommendations validate your skills and achievements, offering third-party verification of your capabilities.
- **Trust:** They instill trust in those viewing your profile, as endorsements from peers carry more weight than self-proclaimed expertise.
- **Visibility:** A well-recommended profile often ranks higher in LinkedIn's search results, making it more discoverable to potential connections and employers.

➤ **Networking:** Recommendations can lead to new opportunities, as they highlight your qualifications and character, attracting opportunities and partnerships.

2. Requesting Recommendations:

To harness recommendations effectively, you need to ask for them. Here's how to do it:

➤ **Choose Wisely:** Select recommenders who know your work well and can speak credibly about your skills and character.

➤ **Personalize Your Request:** Craft a thoughtful and personalized message when requesting recommendations. Explain why you value their input and how their recommendation can benefit both parties.

➤ **Offer Guidance:** It's helpful to suggest specific points or projects you'd like the recommender to highlight. This ensures the recommendation aligns with your professional goals.

3. Giving Recommendations:

LinkedIn's recommendation system operates on a mutual basis, meaning if you give a recommendation, you're more likely to receive one in return. When offering recommendations:

- ➤ **Be Specific:** Provide specific examples of the person's strengths, achievements, and the impact they've had on your professional experience.
- ➤ **Highlight Their Qualities:** Emphasize the qualities or skills that make them a valuable professional. Avoid generic statements.

- ➤ **Maintain Professionalism:** Keep your recommendation focused on their professional attributes, avoiding overly personal or irrelevant information.

4. Showcasing Recommendations:

Once you've received recommendations, display them prominently on your LinkedIn profile:

Feature Top Recommendations: You can choose to showcase the recommendations that best align with your professional goals and brand. Include Them in Your Summary: You can include excerpts from your recommendations in your summary section to make them more visible.

5. Regularly Update Recommendations:

As your career progresses and your skills evolve, it's essential to keep your recommendations up to date. Request new recommendations when you've achieved significant milestones or added new skills.

6. Build on Your Reputation:

Harnessing recommendations is an ongoing process that should complement your reputation-building efforts. Consistently deliver quality work, uphold your professional integrity, and engage with your network.

Recommendations on LinkedIn are not just social endorsements; they are valuable assets that can significantly bolster your professional credibility and trustworthiness. By actively seeking recommendations, giving thoughtful endorsements, and maintaining a strong online presence, you can harness the full potential of recommendations and solidify your professional brand on LinkedIn.

Chapter 3

LinkedIn for Sales and Leads

Using LinkedIn for Sales and Lead Generation: A Comprehensive Guide

LinkedIn is not just a platform for job seekers and professional networking; it's also a goldmine for sales professionals and businesses looking to generate leads and grow their customer base. With over 774 million professionals worldwide, LinkedIn offers a vast pool of potential leads. Here's how to effectively use LinkedIn for sales and lead generation.

1. Optimize Your Profile:

Before you can successfully generate leads on LinkedIn, you need to have a well-optimized profile. This includes a professional profile picture, a compelling headline, and a well-written summary that showcases your expertise and what you offer.

2. Identify Your Target Audience:

Clearly define your ideal customer or client. Understand their industry, job roles, and pain points. This will help you tailor your lead generation efforts.

3. Build a Strong Network:

Connect with professionals who are in your target audience. Start with your existing contacts, and use LinkedIn's search and filter options to find and connect with potential leads.

4. Content Strategy:

Share valuable and relevant content. This positions you as a subject matter expert and keeps your network engaged. Articles, posts, and updates that provide solutions to common industry problems are particularly effective.

5. Engage with Your Network:

Interact with your connections. Comment on their posts, ask questions, and participate in discussions. Engaging with your network builds relationships and keeps you top of mind.

6. Use Advanced Search:

LinkedIn's advanced search features allow you to find prospects based on specific criteria like job title, company, location, and more. It's a powerful tool for finding potential leads.

7. Join and Participate in Groups:

LinkedIn groups are a great way to connect with like-minded professionals. Participate actively, share your expertise, and make connections.

8. Personalized Messaging:

When reaching out to potential leads, always send personalized messages. Explain why you want to connect or how you can provide value to them.

9. Showcase Your Products or Services:

Use LinkedIn's product and services pages to highlight what your business offers. Encourage satisfied clients to leave recommendations.

10. Sponsored Content and Ads:

LinkedIn offers advertising options to promote your business to a targeted audience. Sponsored content and InMail campaigns can be effective for lead generation.

11. Regularly Update Your Profile:

Keep your profile up to date with your latest work and achievements. A professional, updated profile is more likely to attract leads.

12. Analyze and Adjust:

Use LinkedIn's analytics tools to measure the effectiveness of your lead generation efforts. Track metrics like profile views, connection requests, and engagement with your content. Adjust your strategy based on what works.

13. Utilize Sales Navigator:

LinkedIn's Sales Navigator is a premium tool that provides advanced lead generation features. It allows you to save leads, track their activity, and receive lead recommendations.

Prospecting and Connecting on LinkedIn: A Strategic Approach

LinkedIn is a dynamic platform for professional networking and business growth. When used strategically, it can be a valuable resource for prospecting and connecting with potential clients, partners, and leads. Before you begin prospecting, ensure that your LinkedIn profile is well-optimized. A professional profile picture, a compelling headline, and a detailed summary showcasing your expertise are essential elements.

Identify your target audience. Who are your ideal clients or partners? Consider factors like industry, job roles, location, and company size. This clarity will guide your prospecting efforts. Use LinkedIn's advanced search features to find potential prospects. You can search for professionals based on specific criteria such as job title, company, and location. This helps you narrow down your search.

Consider using LinkedIn Premium or Sales Navigator for advanced prospecting. These paid features provide additional filters and tools for more effective lead generation. When sending connection requests, always include a personalized message. Explain why you want to connect and how the connection can be mutually beneficial. A generic request is less likely to be accepted.

Interact with the content shared by your potential prospects. Like, comment, and share their posts to start building a relationship. Engaging with their content shows your genuine interest in their work. Look for mutual connections who can introduce you to your prospects. A warm introduction through a common connection can be more effective than a cold outreach.

Consider using LinkedIn InMail for direct messaging if you're unable to connect through regular means. Keep your InMail concise, personalized, and focused on the recipient's needs or interests. Participate in LinkedIn groups related to your industry or target audience. Engage in discussions and offer valuable insights. This can lead to meaningful connections with like-minded professionals.

Share valuable content to position yourself as an industry expert. This attracts potential prospects who are interested in your field. When someone accepts your connection request, send a thank-you message to express your appreciation for connecting. This helps initiate a positive relationship.

Regularly update and engage with your LinkedIn profile. Consistency is essential in maintaining a strong professional presence. Don't stop at the initial connection. Follow up with your new connections to build a deeper relationship. Engage in meaningful conversations to understand their needs and how you can provide value.

Not all prospects will respond immediately, and some may not respond at all. Be patient and respectful in your interactions, and don't be discouraged by rejection or non-responses. Use LinkedIn analytics to track the effectiveness of your prospecting efforts. Monitor connection acceptance rates, profile views, and engagement with your content. Adjust your strategy based on the data.

In conclusion, prospecting and connecting on LinkedIn is a strategic process that, when done effectively, can lead to valuable business relationships and opportunities. By optimizing your profile, defining your ideal prospects, personalizing your outreach, and engaging with your network, you can harness the full potential of LinkedIn for your professional and business growth.

Managing Your Sales Pipeline on LinkedIn

LinkedIn isn't just a platform for connecting with professionals; it's also a powerful tool for managing your sales pipeline and generating leads. When used strategically, it can help sales professionals and businesses nurture relationships, track opportunities, and ultimately convert leads into customers.

1. Profile Optimization:

Before you begin managing your sales pipeline, ensure your LinkedIn profile is well-optimized. A professional photo, a compelling headline, and a detailed summary highlighting your expertise are crucial elements that make a positive first impression.

2. Define Your Target Audience:

Identify your ideal customer profiles. Who are your target clients or leads? Understand their industry, job roles, and pain points. This will guide your outreach and engagement strategies.

3. Advanced Search and Filters:

Leverage LinkedIn's advanced search and filters to find potential prospects. You can narrow your search by criteria such as location, industry, company size, and job role.

4. Connections and Network Growth:

Build a strong network on LinkedIn. Connect with professionals in your industry and those who fit your target audience. A robust network provides a broader pool of potential leads.

5. Consistent Engagement:

Engage with your connections and network consistently. Like, comment, and share their content, and reach out to start conversations. Regular engagement keeps you visible and reinforces relationships.

6. LinkedIn Groups:

Participate in LinkedIn groups relevant to your industry or target audience. Engage in discussions, offer insights, and build relationships with like-minded professionals.

7. Content Sharing:

Share valuable content that showcases your expertise. This can position you as an industry expert and attract potential leads interested in your field.

8. Personalized Messaging:

When reaching out to potential leads, always send personalized messages. Explain why you want to connect or how you can provide value to them. A personal touch improves your chances of getting a positive response.

9. Use LinkedIn Sales Navigator:

Consider using LinkedIn Sales Navigator, a premium tool that offers advanced lead generation features. It allows you to save leads, track their activity, and receive lead recommendations.

10. Track Leads and Opportunities:

As you connect and engage with potential leads, maintain a system for tracking your interactions. LinkedIn's built-in tagging and notes features can help you stay organized.

11. Set Goals:

Establish clear sales and lead generation goals. Define key performance indicators (KPIs) to measure your progress. These could include connection acceptance rates, message response rates, or lead conversion rates.

12. Relationship Building:

Focus on building genuine relationships rather than rushing to the sale. Engage in meaningful conversations, understand your leads' needs, and tailor your approach accordingly.

13. Use InMail and Messages:

Leverage LinkedIn's messaging features to continue conversations with potential leads. Use InMail and messaging for follow-ups and nurturing relationships.

14. Monitor Analytics:

LinkedIn provides analytics tools to measure the effectiveness of your lead generation efforts. Track metrics like profile views, connection acceptance rates, and engagement with your content. Use this data to refine your strategy.

15. Consistency and Patience:

Sales pipeline management on LinkedIn is an ongoing process. Be consistent with your efforts, and exercise patience. Not all leads will convert immediately, but consistent and thoughtful engagement can yield results over time.

LinkedIn serves as a powerful platform for sales professionals and businesses to grow and prosper in the digital age.

Measuring Sales Success on LinkedIn: Key Metrics and Strategies

LinkedIn has evolved beyond a networking platform into a powerful sales and lead generation tool. Measuring your sales success on LinkedIn is essential to understand the impact of your efforts and refine your strategy. By focusing on key metrics and employing effective strategies, you can gauge your performance and enhance your sales results. To measure your sales success on LinkedIn:

1. Define Your Goals:

Before you start measuring success, it's crucial to establish clear goals. What are you trying to achieve on LinkedIn? Whether it's lead generation, client acquisition, or brand visibility, defining your objectives will guide your measurement efforts.

2. Key Performance Indicators (KPIs):

Determine the KPIs that align with your goals. These may include:

- ➢ **Connection Acceptance Rate:** How many connection requests are accepted compared to the total number sent?
- ➢ **Message Response Rate**: What percentage of your outreach messages receive a response?
- ➢ **Lead Conversion Rate:** How many leads from LinkedIn have turned into actual customers?
- ➢ **Profile Views:** The number of times your profile is viewed, indicating your visibility.
- ➢ **Engagement Metrics:** Measure likes, comments, shares, and click-through rates on your content.

3. LinkedIn Analytics:

LinkedIn offers built-in analytics tools that provide insights into your profile and content performance. Regularly review these metrics to gauge your progress. Pay attention to the performance of specific posts, connection growth, and engagement levels.

4. Profile Views:

The number of profile views is a valuable metric. A higher number indicates increased visibility, but it's essential to assess the quality of those views. Are they from your target audience?

5. Engagement Metrics:

Engagement on your posts and content is an indicator of interest and relevance. Monitor likes, comments, and shares to understand which content resonates with your audience. Adjust your strategy based on these insights.

6. Connection Growth:

The growth of your professional network is an essential metric. However, the quality of your connections matters more than quantity. Are your new connections aligning with your target audience?

7. Message Response Rate:

Track the response rate to your outreach messages. A high response rate indicates effective communication, while a low rate might signal the need for message optimization.

8. Lead Tracking:

For lead generation, track the number of leads that LinkedIn has generated and how many have converted into paying customers. This is a direct measure of sales success.

9. Conversion Rate:

Calculate your lead conversion rate by dividing the number of leads converted into customers by the total number of LinkedIn-generated leads. This provides a clear picture of your conversion efficiency.

10. Content Performance:

Examine the performance of your content, especially if thought leadership and content marketing are part of your strategy. Pay attention to which types of content drive engagement and which fall flat.

11. Follower Growth:

If you manage a LinkedIn company page, monitor follower growth. A growing follower count signifies an expanding audience.

12. Benchmarking:

Compare your LinkedIn metrics to industry benchmarks to understand how your performance measures up. This context can help you set realistic goals and identify areas for improvement.

13. A/B Testing:

Conduct A/B testing on various elements of your LinkedIn strategy, such as message templates, content formats, and posting times. Analyze the data to determine what works best.

14. Continuous Improvement:

Use your metrics to refine your LinkedIn strategy. Identify areas where you can improve and optimize your outreach, content, and engagement to better align with your goals.

In conclusion, measuring sales success on LinkedIn is essential for refining your approach and achieving your goals. By defining clear objectives, focusing on relevant

KPIs, regularly monitoring LinkedIn analytics, and using data-driven insights, you can assess your progress and continuously enhance your performance on this powerful professional networking platform.

Chapter 4

LinkedIn Advertising and Marketing

LinkedIn Advertising and Marketing: Strategies for Success

LinkedIn, with its vast network of over 774 million professionals, offers a unique opportunity for businesses and individuals to reach a highly targeted and professional audience. When harnessed effectively, LinkedIn advertising and marketing can help you promote your brand, generate leads, and establish thought leadership in your industry. Here's a comprehensive guide on how to succeed in LinkedIn advertising and marketing.

LinkedIn Advertising Options:

LinkedIn offers several advertising options to suit different marketing goals:

- ➤ **Sponsored Content:** This format allows you to promote your LinkedIn posts to a broader audience, boosting engagement and visibility.

- ➤ **Sponsored InMail:** A more personalized approach, this format enables you to send tailored messages to a select audience.

- ➤ **Display Ads:** Display ads appear on the LinkedIn homepage, profile pages, and more. They can include images and interactive elements.

- ➤ **Video Ads:** Engaging video content can be used to reach a targeted audience, conveying your message more effectively.

- ➤ **Carousel Ads:** These ads display a series of swipeable cards, each with its own message or image. They are ideal for showcasing multiple products or services.

Define Your Target Audience:

Effective marketing on LinkedIn starts with a deep understanding of your ideal audience. Use LinkedIn's robust targeting options to narrow down your audience by factors such as job title, industry, company size, and location. The more precise your targeting, the more relevant your ads will be to the right people.

Compelling Ad Creative:

Your ad creative should be engaging and resonate with your target audience. Highlight the unique value your product or service offers and craft a compelling call to action (CTA). Visual elements such as eye-catching images, videos, or infographics can make your ad stand out.

Budget and Bidding Strategy:

Determine your advertising budget and bidding strategy. LinkedIn allows you to set daily or lifetime budgets and choose from various bidding options, such as cost per click (CPC) or cost per impression (CPM). Experiment with different strategies to find what works best for your campaign.

Ad Copy and Landing Pages:

Ensure that your ad copy is concise and to the point, delivering a clear message. Your landing page should provide a seamless and relevant experience for users who click on your ad.

A/B Testing:

Experiment with different ad variations to identify what resonates most with your target audience. Test various ad headlines, ad copy, and visuals to optimize your campaign performance.

Conversion Tracking:

Implement conversion tracking on your website to measure the effectiveness of your LinkedIn campaigns. Track metrics such as leads generated, form submissions, or product purchases to assess your ROI.

Sponsored Content:

Sponsored content is a versatile ad format that promotes your LinkedIn posts to a broader audience. Create engaging and informative content that adds value to your target audience. By boosting these posts, you can reach professionals who are likely to engage with your content and, ultimately, your brand.

Sponsored InMail:

Sponsored InMail allows you to send personalized messages to your target audience. Craft a compelling message that addresses the recipient's pain points and offers a solution. Ensure your InMail is concise, engaging, and mobile-friendly.

Display Ads and Video Ads:

Display ads and video ads are visually striking formats that can capture the attention of your audience. Use attention-grabbing visuals and compelling storytelling to convey your message effectively. Consider using video content to engage viewers and tell your brand's story.

Carousel Ads:

Carousel ads are a dynamic way to showcase multiple products or services in a single ad. Each card in the carousel can have its own headline, image, and CTA. Use this format to highlight different offerings and drive engagement.

Analytics and Optimization:

Regularly monitor the performance of your LinkedIn advertising campaigns using LinkedIn's analytics tools. Measure click-through rates, conversion rates, and other relevant metrics to assess the success of your campaigns. Make adjustments based on the data to optimize your campaigns for better results.

Content Marketing on LinkedIn:

In addition to paid advertising, LinkedIn provides opportunities for content marketing. Sharing valuable and relevant content, whether through articles, posts, or documents, can help establish your brand's expertise and engage your target audience organically.

Engagement and Interactions:

Engage with your audience by responding to comments, questions, and messages. Foster discussions and connections to build relationships and enhance your brand's presence on the platform.

Thought Leadership:

Position yourself or your brand as a thought leader in your industry by sharing insightful and valuable content. Write articles, post updates, and engage in discussions to showcase your expertise.

Sponsored Content and Native Ads:

Consider using sponsored content and native ads to promote your thought leadership content to a wider audience. These formats blend seamlessly with users' feeds, increasing the likelihood of engagement.

LinkedIn Groups:

Join and participate in LinkedIn groups relevant to your industry. Engaging in group discussions can help you connect with like-minded professionals and share your expertise.

Data-Driven Approach:

Regularly review the analytics provided by LinkedIn to measure the performance of your content and campaigns. Identify trends and adjust your strategy accordingly to continually improve your marketing efforts.

Engagement and Networking:

Engage with your audience by responding to comments and messages. Networking with peers, clients, and potential leads can strengthen your professional relationships.

Consistency:

Consistency is key to successful marketing on LinkedIn. Regularly post content, engage with your network, and maintain a consistent brand presence on the platform.

Track Results:

Monitor the results of your content marketing efforts. Track metrics such as engagement rates, click-through rates, and follower growth. Use these insights to refine your content strategy.

Sponsored Content and Native Ads:

Consider using sponsored content and native ads to amplify your content's reach. These formats blend seamlessly with users' feeds, increasing the likelihood of engagement.

Analyze and Adjust:

Regularly review your LinkedIn marketing efforts and adjust your strategy based on the performance data and audience feedback. Flexibility and adaptability are essential in maximizing your success on the platform.

Paid Promotion:

To further expand your reach, consider promoting your thought leadership content through paid LinkedIn campaigns. Sponsored content and native ads can increase your content's visibility among your target audience.

Sponsored Content and Ads on LinkedIn

LinkedIn, with its vast network of professionals, offers a unique platform for reaching a highly targeted audience. Sponsored content and ads on LinkedIn allow businesses and individuals to amplify their reach, promote their brand, and generate leads. Understanding how to effectively use these advertising options is key to maximizing your marketing efforts. Here's a comprehensive guide on sponsored content and ads on LinkedIn.

Sponsored Content:

Sponsored content on LinkedIn is a powerful way to reach a broader audience by promoting your organic posts. This ad format appears directly in the LinkedIn feed, offering an unobtrusive way to engage with your target audience. Here are some key considerations for sponsored content:

- **Content Quality:** Start with high-quality content that provides value to your audience. Sponsored content should be informative, engaging, and relevant to your target audience.
- **Audience Targeting:** Utilize LinkedIn's robust targeting options to define your ideal audience. Consider factors like job title, industry, company size, location, and more to reach the right professionals.
- **Clear Call to Action (CTA):** Each sponsored post should include a clear and compelling CTA that guides users to take the desired action, whether it's visiting your website, downloading content, or signing up for an event.

➤ **A/B Testing:** Experiment with different ad variations to identify what resonates most with your target audience. Test various headlines, ad copy, and visuals to optimize your campaign's performance.

➤ **Budget and Bidding:** Set a daily or lifetime budget and choose from different bidding options, such as cost per click (CPC) or cost per impression (CPM). Adjust your budget and bidding strategy based on your campaign goals and performance.

➤ **Performance Tracking:** Regularly monitor the performance of your sponsored content using LinkedIn's analytics tools. Measure click-through rates (CTR), engagement rates, and conversions to assess your campaign's success.

Sponsored InMail:

Sponsored InMail on LinkedIn allows you to send personalized messages directly to the LinkedIn inboxes of your target audience. This ad format is ideal for delivering highly personalized and targeted messages. Here's how to make the most of Sponsored InMail:

➤ **Personalization:** Craft highly personalized messages that address the recipient by name and offer a tailored solution to their specific needs or pain points.

➤ **Engaging Copy:** Ensure your InMail is concise, engaging, and mobile-friendly. Highlight the value you can provide and include a clear CTA.

➤ **Audience Segmentation:** Use LinkedIn's targeting options to segment your audience effectively. Consider factors like job function, company size, and more to reach the most relevant professionals.

- ➢ **Testing and Optimization:** A/B test different message variations to determine which ones perform best. Optimize your Sponsored InMail campaigns based on engagement and conversion data.

- ➢ **Conversion Tracking:** Implement conversion tracking to measure the effectiveness of your Sponsored InMail campaigns. Track metrics like lead generation, form submissions, and event sign-ups.

Display Ads and Video Ads:

Display ads and video ads on LinkedIn offer visually striking formats that can capture the attention of your audience. Use these formats to convey your message effectively and tell your brand's story. Consider these tips for display and video ads:

- ➢ **Attention-Grabbing Visuals:** Create visually appealing ad creatives that stand out in users' feeds. Use compelling images, videos, or infographics to capture attention.

- ➢ **Engaging Storytelling:** Craft compelling stories that resonate with your target audience. Use videos to engage viewers and deliver a memorable message.

- ➢ **Clear CTAs:** Include clear and compelling CTAs in your ad creatives. Encourage users to take action, whether it's visiting your website, downloading content, or making a purchase.

- ➢ **Targeting Options:** Use LinkedIn's targeting options to reach professionals who align with your campaign objectives. Segment your audience by industry, job title, location, and more.

➢ **Performance Metrics:** Monitor performance metrics such as CTR, engagement rates, and conversions to assess the effectiveness of your display and video ad campaigns.

Carousel Ads:

Carousel ads are a dynamic way to showcase multiple products or services in a single ad. Each card in the carousel can have its own headline, image, and CTA.

➢ **Highlight Multiple Offerings:** Use carousel ads to showcase a range of products or services. Each card can represent a different offering, increasing the variety of content users see.

➢ **Engaging Visuals:** Design visually appealing and complementary images for each card in the carousel. Visuals should tell a cohesive story or present a consistent theme.

➢ **Clear CTAs:** Each card should feature a clear CTA that guides users to take action, whether it's learning more, signing up, or making a purchase.

➢ **A/B Testing:** Experiment with different card sequences and content variations to identify which combinations drive the best engagement and conversions.

➢ **Monitoring Performance:** Regularly analyze the performance of your carousel ads using LinkedIn's analytics tools. Assess the CTR, engagement rates, and conversions for each card in the carousel.

Content Marketing on LinkedIn:

In addition to paid advertising, LinkedIn provides opportunities for content marketing. Sharing valuable and relevant content, whether through articles, posts, or documents, can help establish your brand's expertise and engage your target audience organically. Here's how to succeed in content marketing on LinkedIn:

➢ **Thoughtful Leadership:** Position yourself or your brand as a thoughtful leader in your industry. Share insightful and valuable content, write articles, post updates, and engage in discussions to showcase your expertise.

➢ **Engaging Content:** Create content that resonates with your audience. Share industry insights, success stories, practical tips, and thought-provoking ideas.

➢ **Consistency:** Maintain a consistent posting schedule to keep your audience engaged and looking forward to your content. Regular posting helps strengthen your brand presence on the platform.

➢ **A/B Testing:** Experiment with different types of content, posting times, and messaging approaches to understand what works best for your audience.

➢ **Engagement and Networking:** Engage with your audience by responding to comments, questions, and messages. Foster discussions and connections to build relationships and enhance your brand's presence on the platform.

➢ **Content Promotion:** Use sponsored content and native ads to promote your thought leadership content to a wider audience. These formats blend seamlessly with users' feeds, increasing the likelihood of engagement.

➢ **LinkedIn Groups:** Join and participate in LinkedIn groups relevant to your industry. Engaging in group discussions can help you connect with like-minded professionals and share your expertise.

Data-Driven Approach:

Regularly review the analytics provided by LinkedIn to measure the performance of your content and campaigns. Identify trends and adjust your strategy accordingly to continually improve your marketing efforts.

Engagement and Networking:

Engage with your audience by responding to comments and messages. Networking with peers, clients, and potential leads can strengthen your professional relationships.

Consistency:

Consistency is key to successful marketing on LinkedIn. Regularly post content, engage with your network, and maintain a consistent brand presence on the platform.

Track Results:

Monitor the results of your content marketing efforts. Track metrics such as engagement rates, click-through rates, and follower growth. Use these insights to refine your content strategy.

Sponsored Content and Native Ads:

Consider using sponsored content and native ads to amplify your content's reach. These formats blend seamlessly with users' feeds, increasing the likelihood of engagement.

Analyze and Adjust:

Regularly review your LinkedIn marketing efforts and adjust your strategy based on the performance data and audience feedback. Flexibility and adaptability are essential in maximizing your success on the platform.

In conclusion, sponsored content and ads on LinkedIn offer a range of options to promote your brand, generate leads, and establish thought leadership. By crafting engaging ad creatives, setting clear CTAs, targeting the right audience, and monitoring performance metrics, you can achieve success in your LinkedIn advertising and marketing campaigns. Additionally, content marketing on LinkedIn allows you to organically engage your audience and position yourself as a thought leader in your industry. Using data-driven insights, fostering engagement, and maintaining consistency are key to achieving your marketing goals on this professional networking platform.

Company Pages and Showcase on LinkedIn: A Guide to Effective Brand Promotion

Company Pages and Showcase Pages on LinkedIn serve as powerful tools for businesses and organizations to establish their presence, promote their brand, and engage with a professional audience. These platforms allow companies to share their story, showcase their products or services, and connect with customers, partners, and potential employees.

Company Pages are the primary brand presence on LinkedIn. They provide an overview of your organization, its mission, and its offerings. Here's how to make the most of your Company Page:

Optimize the Profile: Ensure your Company Page is complete with a professional logo, a compelling banner image, and a concise yet informative description of your business.

Engaging Content: Regularly post updates, articles, and content that reflects your brand's values and expertise. Share industry insights, company news, and success stories.

Visual Elements: Use images and videos to enhance your posts. Visual content tends to attract more engagement and can help convey your brand's story effectively.

Target Audience: Define your target audience on LinkedIn and tailor your content to their interests and needs. Consider factors like industry, job roles, and location when curating content.

Employee Advocacy: Encourage your employees to link to the Company Page in their profiles and share company updates. Employee advocacy can significantly amplify your brand's reach.

Engagement and Networking: Respond to comments, messages, and connection requests promptly. Engage with your audience to build relationships and foster a sense of community around your brand.

Analytics and Optimization: Utilize LinkedIn's analytics tools to monitor the performance of your Company Page. Track metrics like follower growth, post engagement, and click-through rates to evaluate your impact.

Showcase Pages:

Showcase Pages are extensions of your Company Page and allow you to highlight specific aspects of your business. These pages are ideal for showcasing individual brands, products, services, or initiatives. Here's how to maximize the potential of Showcase Pages:

Clear Branding: Ensure that each Showcase Page maintains consistent branding with your Company Page. Use the same logo and banner design to establish brand recognition.

Focused Content: Tailor the content on each Showcase Page to the specific product, service, or initiative it represents. Share updates, case studies, and industry insights related to that particular aspect of your business.

Targeted Audience: Define the target audience for each Showcase Page, and adjust your content and messaging accordingly. This ensures that you're reaching the right professionals interested in that area.

Employee Involvement: Encourage employees with expertise in the area of the Showcase Page to contribute content and engage with the audience. Employee participation adds authenticity and depth to your brand's presence.

Consistency and Variety: Regularly update the content on your Showcase Pages to keep the audience engaged. Include a mix of posts, articles, videos, and visuals to provide a well-rounded view of the highlighted aspect.

Cross-Promotion: Promote your Showcase Pages on your Company Page and through your other marketing channels to increase visibility and followers.

Analytics and Optimization: Use LinkedIn's analytics tools to track the performance of your Showcase Pages. Monitor metrics like follower growth, engagement rates, and content impact. Adjust your strategy based on the data.

LinkedIn Events:

LinkedIn Events provide an additional dimension to your brand promotion efforts. They allow you to create and promote events such as webinars, product launches, workshops, and conferences.

Event Creation: Create compelling event listings, including event details, descriptions, dates, and registration links. Use engaging visuals and clear, informative titles.

Promotion: Promote your events on both your Company Page and Showcase Pages to maximize visibility. Encourage employees and followers to share the event with their networks.

Networking: Engage with event attendees through comments, messages, and discussions. Foster connections and build relationships around your events.

Feedback and Follow-Up: Collect feedback from event attendees to evaluate your event's success. Follow up with participants to maintain relationships and encourage further engagement with your brand.

Analytics and Optimization: Use LinkedIn's event analytics to assess the performance of your events. Monitor metrics like registration rates, attendee engagement, and post-event interactions.

Content Marketing:

Incorporate content marketing strategies into your Company Page, Showcase Pages, and LinkedIn Events to provide valuable and relevant information to your audience. Share industry insights, thoughtful leadership articles, success stories, and practical tips.

Regular Posting: Maintain a consistent posting schedule to keep your audience engaged. Post updates, articles, and visuals that reflect your brand's values and expertise.

Thoughtful Leadership: Position your brand as a thought leader in your industry by sharing insightful content and engaging in discussions.

Engagement: Respond to comments and messages promptly, and encourage discussions around your content. Engagement fosters a sense of community and strengthens your brand presence.

Sponsored Content: Consider using sponsored content and native ads to promote your thought leadership content to a wider audience. These formats blend seamlessly with users' feeds, increasing the likelihood of engagement.

In conclusion, Company Pages, Showcase Pages, and LinkedIn Events provide a comprehensive platform for businesses to promote their brand and engage with a professional audience. By optimizing your profile, crafting engaging content, targeting the right audience, and monitoring performance metrics, you can effectively leverage LinkedIn's tools for brand promotion and growth. Additionally, integrating content marketing strategies into your LinkedIn presence allows you to provide value to your audience and establish your brand as a thought leader in your industry.

Event and Group Marketing on LinkedIn: Building Communities and Engagement

LinkedIn offers a valuable platform for event and group marketing, allowing businesses and professionals to connect with their target audience, foster communities, and drive engagement. By effectively utilizing these features, you can not only promote your brand but also create a space for meaningful interactions.

Event Marketing:

LinkedIn Events provide a platform for promoting and managing various gatherings, from webinars and conferences to product launches and networking sessions

1. Event Creation:

Create compelling event listings that include event details, descriptions, dates, and registration links. Use engaging visuals and clear, informative titles to make your event stand out.

2. Promotion:

Promote your events on your Company Page, Showcase Pages, and personal profiles. Encourage your employees and followers to share the event with their networks to maximize visibility.

3. Networking:

Engage with event attendees through comments, messages, and discussions. Create a space for participants to interact and connect with one another, fostering relationships and strengthening their connection to your brand.

4. Feedback and Follow-Up:

Collect feedback from event attendees to evaluate your event's success and gather insights for improvement. Follow up with participants after the event to maintain relationships and encourage further engagement with your brand.

5. Analytics and Optimization:

Utilize LinkedIn's event analytics to assess the performance of your events. Monitor metrics such as registration rates, attendee engagement, and post-event interactions. Use these insights to refine your future event marketing strategies.

Group Marketing:

LinkedIn Groups are communities where professionals with common interests or goals can engage in discussions and share insights. Leveraging groups effectively can help you build your brand's presence, connect with your audience, and establish thoughtful leadership.

Consider creating a LinkedIn Group that aligns with your brand's industry or niche. This group can serve as a hub for discussions, networking, and knowledge sharing. Ensure the group's name and description are clear and relevant.

Share valuable content within your group, such as industry insights, thought leadership articles, success stories, and practical tips. Content should be relevant to the group's interests and encourage discussions.

Foster discussions and interactions within your group by actively engaging with members. Respond to comments, ask questions, and initiate conversations. Ensure the group remains a positive and valuable space by moderating and removing spam or irrelevant content.

Position your brand as a thoughtful leader by sharing insightful content and engaging in discussions. Encourage your employees to participate and contribute their expertise to the group.

LinkedIn Groups provide an excellent platform for networking. Engage with group members and connect with those who align with your brand's goals. Building professional relationships within the group can lead to meaningful connections and opportunities.

Utilize group analytics to assess the performance of your LinkedIn Group. Track metrics like member growth, engagement rates, and content impact. Adjust your group's strategy based on the data to keep members engaged and foster a vibrant community. Consider using sponsored content and native ads to promote your group or group-related content to a wider LinkedIn audience. These formats blend seamlessly with users' feeds, increasing the likelihood of engagement.

By creating compelling events, promoting them effectively, and fostering meaningful interactions, you can not only promote your brand but also create spaces for valuable connections. Similarly, by establishing and managing LinkedIn Groups that encourage discussions, knowledge sharing, and networking, you can establish your brand as a thought leader and build a thriving community. Leveraging sponsored content and native ads can also extend your reach and bring your event or group to a broader audience. With consistent effort and data-driven optimization, event and group marketing on LinkedIn can be a cornerstone of your brand's online presence and engagement strategy.

Frequently Asked Questions (FAQS)

Here are 20 frequently asked questions about LinkedIn, along with appropriate answers:

What is LinkedIn?

- ✓ LinkedIn is a professional social networking platform used for business and career development.

Is LinkedIn free to use?

- ✓ Yes, LinkedIn offers a free basic account, but there are premium subscription options with additional features.

How do I create a LinkedIn profile?

- ✓ To create a profile, visit LinkedIn.com, click "Join now," and follow the prompts to enter your information.

What should I include in my LinkedIn profile summary?

- ✓ Your summary should highlight your professional background, skills, and career goals.

How do I connect with people on LinkedIn?

- ✓ You can send connection requests to individuals you know or want to network with.

What's the difference between "connections" and "followers" on LinkedIn?

- ✓ Connections are mutual relationships, while followers are people who follow your updates but may not be connected directly.

How can I optimize my LinkedIn profile for job searching?

✓ Use a professional photo, add a compelling headline, and include relevant keywords in your profile.

Can I apply for jobs directly through LinkedIn?

✓ Yes, you can apply for jobs through LinkedIn's job postings or through the Easy Apply feature.

How can I request recommendations from my connections?

✓ You can send a request for a recommendation from your connections, specifying what you'd like them to highlight.

What's the purpose of LinkedIn endorsements?

✓ Endorsements allow your connections to confirm your skills and expertise, enhancing your profile's credibility.

How can I search for job opportunities on LinkedIn?

✓ You can use the job search feature to filter and find relevant job postings.

Is it appropriate to message people I don't know on LinkedIn?

✓ It's acceptable to send a polite and professional message to network or inquire about job opportunities, but be respectful of their time.

What's the best way to utilize LinkedIn for networking?

✓ Join relevant groups, participate in discussions, and attend virtual or in-person networking events.

Can I share personal updates on LinkedIn, or is it just for professional content?

✓ While LinkedIn is primarily for professional content, it's acceptable to share some personal achievements or career-related updates.

How can I showcase my work on my LinkedIn profile?

✓ You can use the "Featured" section to display articles, presentations, and other work samples.

Are there privacy settings on LinkedIn to control who sees my information?

✓ Yes, you can adjust your privacy settings to control what information is visible to others.

How can I stand out to recruiters on LinkedIn?

✓ Make sure your profile is complete, and engage with relevant industry content to increase your visibility.

Is LinkedIn beneficial for freelancers and entrepreneurs?

✓ Yes, LinkedIn can be a valuable platform for networking, finding clients, and building your personal brand.

What's the ideal frequency for posting content on LinkedIn?

✓ Posting 2-3 times per week is a good starting point, but consistency and quality matter more than frequency.

Can I use LinkedIn for learning and professional development?

✓ Yes, LinkedIn offers LinkedIn Learning with various courses and resources to help you improve your skills and knowledge.

How can I delete my LinkedIn account?

✓ To delete your LinkedIn account, go to "Settings & Privacy," then "Account preferences," and select "Account management." Follow the prompts to close your account.

What is the "All-Star" status on LinkedIn, and how can I achieve it?

✓ The "All-Star" status is LinkedIn's highest profile strength. You can achieve it by adding a professional photo, a headline, a summary, work experience, education, and skills to your profile.

Is it necessary to customize my LinkedIn URL?

✓ Customizing your LinkedIn URL makes it more professional and easier to share. You can do this in the "Edit public profile & URL" section.

How can I get noticed by recruiters on LinkedIn?

✓ You can optimize your profile with relevant keywords, engage with industry-related content, and let recruiters know you're open to new opportunities in your settings.

Can I endorse someone I haven't worked with directly?

✓ While it's best to endorse people you've worked with, you can endorse others if you genuinely believe they possess the skills you're endorsing.

Is it acceptable to connect with someone and then immediately ask for a job referral?

✓ It's more effective to build a relationship with your connections before requesting job referrals or recommendations.

How can I make my LinkedIn profile more visually appealing?

✓ You can add a background photo, upload media to the "Featured" section, and use bullet points and whitespace in your job descriptions to make your profile visually appealing.

Can I use LinkedIn for B2B (business-to-business) marketing?

✓ Yes, LinkedIn is a valuable platform for B2B marketing, allowing you to target specific industries and professionals through advertising and content sharing.

What's the etiquette for endorsing a colleague for skills they don't possess?

✓ It's essential to endorse your connections honestly. Endorsing skills they don't have may harm your professional credibility.

Is it acceptable to post job-related content on my personal LinkedIn profile?

✓ Yes, sharing relevant job-related content, such as industry news or job openings, can demonstrate your expertise and help your network.

How can I request introductions to second-degree connections on LinkedIn?

✓ You can ask your mutual connection for an introduction or send a connection request to the second-degree connection with a personalized message.

Are LinkedIn Premium subscriptions worth the cost?

✓ The value of LinkedIn Premium depends on your specific goals. It can provide additional features, such as InMail and advanced search filters, which can be useful for job seekers and network builders.

Can I use LinkedIn to find freelance or remote work opportunities?

✓ Yes, many companies and clients post freelance and remote job opportunities on LinkedIn. You can use specific filters in the job search to find these types of roles.

Is it okay to connect with my current colleagues on LinkedIn?

✓ Yes, it's common and acceptable to connect with current colleagues, as it can help you stay connected and share professional updates.

How can I network with industry leaders and influencers on LinkedIn?

✓ Engage with their content, leave thoughtful comments, and send personalized connection requests explaining why you'd like to connect.

Can I share my LinkedIn connections' contact information with others?

✓ It's best to respect your connections' privacy. Sharing their contact information without their consent is generally not recommended.

Is it advisable to include personal interests and hobbies on my LinkedIn profile?

✓ Including personal interests and hobbies can provide a more well-rounded view of your personality but focus primarily on professional information.

How can I keep my LinkedIn network engaged with my profile?

✓ Regularly share meaningful content, engage with your network's updates, and offer value through your posts and discussions.

What should I do if someone sends me an inappropriate message on LinkedIn?

✓ You can report the message and block the user to prevent further contact. LinkedIn takes inappropriate behavior seriously.

How do I request recommendations from former employers or supervisors?

✓ Politely reach out to them and explain why you'd appreciate a recommendation. It's helpful to offer to reciprocate or provide guidance on what you'd like them to highlight.

www.ingramcontent.com/pod-product-compliance
Lightning Source LLC
Chambersburg PA
CBHW082148290526

45794CB00008B/3203